Winter Count Poems

Charles G. Ballard

The Greenfield Review Press

Publication of this book has been made possible by a grant from the Lannan Foundation.

Winter Count Poems by Charles G. Ballard

Copyright 1997 by Charles G. Ballard

All rights reserved. No part of this publication may be reproduced, stored in a retrieval system, or transmitted, in any form by any means, electronic, mechanical, photo copying or otherwise, without the prior written permission of the author.

Grateful acknowledgment is made to the following publications where the following poems first appeared. "The Conference" in *Platte Valley Review* 19.1 (1991):97-8, and "Farmers" in *English Journal*, 79.6 (1990): 95. In *Voices from Wah-kon-tah: Contemporary Poetry and Native Americans*, Robert K. Dodge and Joseph B. McCullough, eds. (New York: International Publishers, 1974), the following appeared: "Navajo Girl of Many Farms," "Changing of the Guard," "Time Was the Trail Went Deep," and "Now the People Have the Light." In *Voices of the Rainbow: Contemporary Poetry by American Indians*, Kenneth Rosen, ed. (New York: Viking Press, 1975), the following poems were published: "Their Cone-Like Cabins," "Grandma Fire," "Memo," "The Spirit Craft," and "During the Pageant at Medicine Lodge." Finally, two poems appeared in *Studies in American Indian Literature* (SAIL): "Outdoor Cafe" and "Kamchatka."

ISBN 0-912678-96-8

Library of Congress Number: 97-70244

Design and composition of cover and text by
Sans Serif Inc., Saline, MI
Printed by MacNaughton & Gunn, Saline, MI

The Greenfield Review Press
Greenfield Center, New York 12833

Distributed by The Talman Company, Inc.
131 Spring St.
New York, NY 10012

For Marilyn and for Laurence, Jo, and Lawson

Contents

We Who Have Traveled Long Distances

Kamchatka   *3*
Outdoor Cafe   *4*
White Eagle   *5*
The Sweet Grass Burns   *6*
Winter Count   *7*
West of Eden   *8*
Business   *9*
Dust Bowl Days   *10*
The Farm   *11*
The Anarchist   *12*

House of Dreams

The House of Dreams   *17*
Cold Spring   *18*
Milton   *19*
Museums   *20*
The Gardener   *21*
Picasso's The Acrobat's Family   *22*
Sir Thomas Wyatt, 1503–1542   *24*
Farmers   *25*
The Book of Fall   *26*
The Old Crew   *27*
Reflections   *28*
By the Lake   *29*

The Austerlitz Station

Journey to Madrid   *33*
Shout Amen   *35*
Christmas Eve   *36*

Lamb without Guile   *37*
Western Gate   *38*
Boulevard   *39*
The Conference   *40*
Millennium   *42*
Austerlitz Station   *43*
Hermeneutic Circles   *44*
The Keys   *45*

Early Poems

Navajo Girl of Many Farms   *49*
During the Pageant at Medicine Lodge   *50*
Now the People Have the Light   *51*
Changing of the Guard   *52*
Grandma Fire   *53*
The Spirit Craft   *54*
Their Cone-Like Cabins   *55*
Memo   *56*
Time Was the Trail Went Deep   *57*

We Who Have Traveled Long Distances

Kamchatka

Ravens circling in a desolate sky,
Moving from a low line of hills
Down to a narrow sandy shore.
Today my thoughts once more
Are on the holy fires of snow-bound
Kamchatka—a faraway land
That is not mine except
By scholar's rights, since I
Have seen it often in my mind,
Have endlessly poured over tomes
In corners of libraries and
Have imagined life, portions of life,
Clinging, burrowing in dark sand
Near its feral, inhospitable dunes,
Near its tangled hills, its narrow streams,
Wondering how in that first dawn
We began to move—move slowly,
Sullenly, gladly, or with resignation
Across the straits to a strange new world.

Outdoor Cafe

Did we not meet
Once upon an ancient bridge
Or upon a winding street?
Yet somewhere as summer came to an end,
With days sputtering to a close,
As the night air carried our word
Beneath the cafe lights,
Burning just within as we sat
And talked, saying once again
What seasons or the years would bring,
What time was about, and why,
With hardly a smile, we would part
As friends, you and I, and that
Would be it—each moment without
Regard to the next, and the past
Also an empty glass beside an empty seat
At an outdoor cafe, now left
For others to rearrange, to play
The songs, to pick up the refrain—
For we have said goodbye and are gone.

White Eagle

We stood beneath the canvas roof
Of a vendor's booth when the rain
In large drops came. We seemed waiting
In a dream, or in an open field
Where only a few lights shown,
Where there were cars, where the young called
Out, covering their heads, shouting
To friends, flashlights waving beneath
Trees, signaling others to come,
To join their crowd, to wave and fly,
All in unexplained merriment,
watching the few who took their chance,
Then bolted, leaving us listening
To the thunderous rain, drenching
Cars, stadium, grounds, everyone
Who had traveled long distances
Expecting the arms of women,
Friends, the end of torment, madness,
And not to be herded like cattle
Into a pen—and by ourselves.
We must be crazy to be here.
The feeling, oh, just to belong,
A blight, a darkness in our soul.
I agreed. These are the nightmare years.
If only morning would soon arrive.

The Sweet Grass Burns

As the snows of another year arrive,
The funeral bells do not toll for him
Or us, nor does the golden bird of dreams
Dispel our doubts that we will yet survive.
The sweet grass burns in service for the few,
Northern winds return to the River Platte,
Who knows the road, or speaks now of the path?
What songs fill the void and what words renew?
The countenance of our world is the past;
We feel the land, we allotted ones, towns
And countryside, we hear the moon but now
Only the roar of time moving at last
Somehow apart from us and all we are—
We who live near a small and single star.

Winter Count

The leaves this year did not fall
because of the early cold
Neither was wood stacked near the house
to bring in for the winter fires
The sky was overcast for days on end
in spite of our prayers for relief
Animals from beyond the barn
paid us several nightly visits
and a stranger one cold afternoon
came by the house when I was alone
He asked if my parents were home
but his face was different, unshaved
and he had walked from the woods
to the house and out there I knew
the trails, the river banks, and the wild
So I held my hand tight to the door
and would not let him in. He
did not explain but simply turned
and braced himself in the bitter wind
Later that year he pointed me out
as the boy who stood at the door
Adults they were and at a handgame
It was the year when a stranger
came to our door, then left.

West of Eden

So begins today on a street roped off
Downtown a protest with shouts
And crowds and cops—an aria
Of spring, which having sprung, sings out,
Using the spice of fermenting doubts
And the nation's holy name, while media
Record and stroll, observing always smoke
And tears near the cauldron of oaths
As visions spring to life or ideas die.
Who knows? Who cares? The people sigh,
Then jeer, then break into applause.
I, too, am happy as a dog. It's fun
Living here with the ghosts of old Cain
And Abel, honking horns, all west of Eden.

Business

South of town a store that sells knicky-knacky
Dinky little things, cups and perfumes,
Ornaments for our Tannenbaum.
Individualism, it says, costs less
Than you think. A vast river of lies
And merchandise and necessities crosses
The land. This large warehouse place invites
Customers to indulge themselves modestly
Because nothing costs much and products
Come from the four corners of our world:
Mountain ranges condensed or boxed,
Animals carefully wrapped, incense
From the Orient, socks, neckerchiefs,
Indian chiefs, wood trains, junk food,
A veritable cornucopia of ideas.
I know this ocean of business
Will expand and one day you may buy
A few lines of a poem by me, stuck
Inside the lid of a music box
("In our hearts the song never ends")
But without a name or a picture
Of my portliness, not even a smile,
Just these few words as though
From a strange voice long ago.
We artists, you see, contributed
To this big pile. You should realize that:
Don't plump down your quarters
And walk out. Turn around, blow us
A kiss, stomp your feet, well, you know,
your turn is coming—look about,
We're up to our ears in it.

Dust Bowl Days

"The Sheik of Araby" was also a hit
On the res, so I hear, but how
would I know? Perhaps everywhere
The whole rural clan went wild
About Rudolph and hummed or went
Into shock while shucking corn,
Sewing quilts, feeding the chicks.
One page had been turned near the end
Of those dust bowl days, new hope
Or fantasy for Auntie in middle age,
While living on next to nothing
In a two-room shack at the edge
Of town, singing "I'm the Sheik of Araby"—
Yeah!

The Farm

In the coolness of morning we started out.
The sun was not yet clear of a line
of hills to the east, the fences still
heavy with dew, and beyond the trees
we heard as a low hum the river
rapids and in the fields the calls
of birds, but mostly we heard
our steps on rocks, on gravel, on earth.
Turning back I could see in the still
dim light the dark room above
the porch where my few possessions were—
clothes, books, model planes, earliest
memories—where seasons and days
filled in the words, the time I had left,
although I saw it always as mostly
a gala affair, happiness for the most part,
one green inviting trail through summer
heat, one matchless path across snow-
covered fields with five protective dogs—
what more could a growing boy request
than open space, a river, a farm
with real wasps and snakes in the grass.

The Anarchist

In that school upon the hill
I was a caustic man, ambling
with a half-smile down corridors,
My flame of life burning thin
As I scurried away at five
To an upstairs room beyond
The shopping malls, the viaduct.
A teacher of youth misguided
But wide-eyed and taciturn,
Coming from arid lands,
From Indian towns. I knew
In my simple room that I was
An anarchist, an anarchist
Entrenched, deep down, but without
Crowds, without the closeness of evil.
I was immobilized, planted deep,
Wondering how I had managed
Open skies, trees, harmless classrooms,
Talkative colleagues, dinner at six,
Chapel every other week. On my walls
A picture of Charles and Di—and
A rhinoceros. Celebrate, I whispered,
The high, the unusual, the proud,
The durable. Try not to be a bomb
And so depart this realm in a cloud
of dust, but bumble on, wait it out
And hold securely in your hand
The match, the fuse that will rain
Hell fire and general destruction

Upon all Christian lands.
Then, at peaceful ground zero,
Or in classrooms, we can start again.

House of Dreams

The House of Dreams

When we were young and cheerful
At the bandstand near the swings,
We jumped with a shout into Time's
Old hamper, watching our bird-
Shadows fly, and these shadows,
I say, began to lengthen
As the seasons began to die.
Life we said was golden,
or muttering and spinning like a top
As we picked out the flavors
And refused to stop: our silver
Names in the House of Dreams.
I believe it was near the city park.
The leaves of autumn gathered
In a heap: we called it now
A gesture and made a toast,
Saying promises were also these,
Or like the summer rose.
Who wins the prize when the die
is cast? Who matters most
When summer comes again?
We lift our glass to better days,
To the wine of youth, to the bitter cold.
Take part in that and use it all,
The candied epithets, the touch
Of frosty lips in days rushing by.
Take part in celebrations
Of the storm before the songs
Of evening fade and are no more.

Cold Spring

I revisit in a field beyond the house
A small spring after years have gone.
Once more I listen to it say,
My name is Green Song, for I
Am an artery of life, or my name
Is Wheel or Mountain-Eater.
When last you were here
The world was a magical place.
Now you have changed. The boy
Has gone his way.
It is true,
I replied, but thoughts also grow,
Insights must be gathered
Far and wide. The clear gushing spring—
You, too, survive as memory,
But it means, I believe, that we
Have merely traveled from our source
And sometimes, as it were, revisit our
Nesting place, our first universe.

Milton

A small wooden bust of who else, Milton,
Who would have banished me, no doubt, heathen
Unbeliever, half-dressed, and countenance
Of wolf, newly arrived in London town.
Carved his head for my desk, the Puritan
Who puzzles me, attracts me, Indian
Of these disjointed times, because reason,
It seems, has emptied us, the souls of men.
And did we speak like that? Heavy Latin
And Greek, solid erudition, and sin
All bubbling up for the American
To consider or forget—and begin
Once more upon another quest—hold firm
At all costs while the roof is caving in.

Museums

Somewhere beyond the great Divide
Where memories and events are lost,
Old pots and old dreams, down
They fell, the laundry chute, twisted
Thongs, burning sage—disappeared
one day into a great museum.
I saw the parts, remains, artifacts,
Bits of life now dreaming upon a shelf,
The world of notes, a world of glass—
Ideas like clouds moving in and out.
Echoes, too. No one around. *I am one
of you.* Believe me, you have a visitor
Quite unique—with mountain streams
Somehow in my breath, an Indian
Through and through, or at least
So once I thought. Old ducks
And little words in a book tried
To tell me I was not. Tried to say
That that life was gone—here's the proof.
You will walk out of this windless room
And stand in the light of day.
Will you leave behind something
Of what you are? The medicine song—
So that to this dark place
You can say goodbye.

The Gardener

The gardener has a knowledge of roots
Events that happen always in the soil,
The structures unseen, tilting of the globe,
Darkness subject to nutrients and light.
Each year a remarkable rose comes forth;
We then believe it represents the truth,
That is, unto itself, and from the Earth,
Which also rides upon a longer course.
So to be ourselves is a dilemma
For some who always ask where we have been,
Where tomorrow is taking us and why.
Of course, like being in a cinema
The questions can suggest and entertain,
But reality? Only if whales fly.

Picasso's the Acrobat's Family

With a Monkey—or so the guidebook says
And there on the wall it hangs.
Notice the feet of the parents resting
So symmetrically in what seems
A bird-like pose, the infant twisting
In its mother's arms—eyes
Of the child looking out from the scene,
Perhaps into the distant years.
Peering deeper, I think a restlessness
Of spirit is here and also much else.
The painting comes, we read, from an earlier time
In the life of the artist, as well as from
That world surrounding the inland sea.
Yet beyond the blooms of color
And seating figures, there are also sounds
Imaginary, crowds stirring, noise
Of the street, the smell of leather and hay,
All mixing with commerce and peels
Of laughter at the crossroads, and again
Messages and words from the rugged hue—
Sand and tides, light pressing steadily down
On hovel and city gate, on epics
And songs that speak of grazing herds,
Temperamental gods, sacred streams,
The firmament above the acropolis:
A world giving way to another world.
And now, strangely enough, circus people
Working at their trade, their lives
Never very calm yet picking up perhaps

The older theme—one family drawing close
As it once did somewhere in Galilee.
Look again at the father's hat,
So loosely there, perhaps with fatigue.
One wonders what it says—something
Not good about our age, I don't know what:
That ridiculous villages have arisen,
Have passed, all overlaid with the new.
And still the monkey only waits, seeing
The family scene and trying to say
That finally not much has changed
Or has moved in these many years.

Sir Thomas Wyatt, 1503–1542

Soldier of the realm and no doubt
Much else, but these have passed
And sentiments expressed
Are mostly words becoming small
In the long gaze of history,
Except, well, for a phrase, a thought,
A voice, or a gentle sigh,
Saying that Vanity's unsightly web
Hath caught but laughter from the wise
Or tears from those with a fragile mind.
So what more is there to add?
The queen of night still softly spins
And will continue to the end.
Enough, I suppose, if old ideas
Have countenance and also mirth,
A seemly rhyme and a simple truth
Fashioned then to survive a silent earth.

Farmers

Heat haze lifting from fields
On a summer afternoon

Thin waves shimmering up
Moving softly in the sun

Ripe bent grain and the trees
High and silent along the road

Stillness, dust, long fences
Drawing all into the barns

Cool darkness where the god
Or gods erstwhile congregate

And barefoot as a child
I watched the great seasons pass

Listened to words and felt
Earth warming beneath my feet

Sheets of rain and the life blood
Of land and the farming life

Hold, then, to the breaking day
As it moves to twilight shade

Study the patterns of light
And wait before you decide.

The Book of Fall

Through a clear gushing spring I walked
On pebbles and on mossy rock
Leaving no traces along the edges
Where ripples spread on waters dark.
The tree above and the fields beyond
Waited, too, till I was gone.
What visions here will break the mold
When the nuthatch comes and the crow,
When summer comes and river shade
Invites the serpent and the toad?
Then all will tarry for a while
To read the Book of Fall and the scents,
Earth-filled messages and the pile
Of leaves now forming by the brook.
Where are you in this silent roar,
This symphony of subtle smells
Along the river trails of earth?
While all tomorrows are splashing
From the pool, or down-rocking, gliding soft
Without seeming to stop, to cease,
Without saying a word, a word.

The Old Crew

I have lost my savoir faire;
Yesterday among the crowd I noticed
It was no longer there.
I have dropped my p's and q's,
Her hand in mine and then
So close, but I suppose old news
To the hometown crowd.
We were the youth, those
Who would succeed, being success-prone,
Or not likely to fail, so someone said.
But so we did, and not just once
Or twice—some hit the skids
And some were not so nice.
We saw less of hometown sights
After divorces or when the retarded
Became people of means, when the wise
Became sad, when the innocent
At last spoke out, mouthing lost causes,
Waiting for rewards, for happiness,
For applause. The gamut of days.
But some there were who drifted
Into quiet harbors where they set up shop
And talked and moved and then moved
Back, where they stayed, raising
Their offspring one by one until they
Simply died, it seemed, of old age.

Reflections

She fell into mountain air far below
Where heather and flowers grow
No doubt beside the Irish Sea
Do not ask her name or disturb her rest
In death the turmoil of her life
Became forever lost as a button
Or a thread is dropped unseen
And spirit or essence is released,
Released, it seems to the universe,
The trackless stars and oblivion.
She herself pushed aside the veil
And so became the thin, silent wing
That moves through the mystic cloud.
Is there music in that beyond
Where time stands still? Are there thoughts
of us as we pace and fret? Is
The crossing all there is and no more?
Do even our questions, like sparrows,
Finally drop beside the massive wall?

By the Lake

The young man looked idly across the lake,
Listening as a young girl spoke, her words
Dreaming almost as she recalled people,
The market place, the journey between towns,
And what she saw:
How charming friends sometimes are
Or how bright sometimes the world
Seems to be, but for us there are
All too few hours in the day,
Too few days in this summer now passing.
This breeze, this view of the bridge, the house,
This rustling of leaves overhead, this grass
So cool to the touch, and also your hand.
We cannot keep this moment, I know, it
Will fly away like the swans and with youth
And days and our promises on their wings.
Who could possibly know just how we felt
Or what our lives, to us, seem to be?
You in your music must be always light
And gay, wild and somehow young so that
Time becomes a ribbon or a book that speaks
Of now, this moment, this touch on your cheek.
Our love must not be a secret but be told
To the world, or at least every time someone
Turns a page and says, Domenico Scarlatti.

The Austerlitz Station

Journey to Madrid

You climb this monstrous hill each morning
to reach the Union and other buildings
of the university. First trial or test
for job-seekers—I miserably failed;
panting like a dog, leaning with one arm
on the wall. Another interview
with Basque professor from, he said, Irun.
That place, too, was atop a hill.
Stop me, I said to myself—the man
thought no one had so much as heard of it.
Pyrenees, near Hendaye, southern France.
Atlantic white caps in the distance
and an expanse of blue. An hour or so
at an outdoor cafe I waited, thinking
what to do. At the border I watched
the Civil Guard inspect people, packages
(These in the days of Franco), and I
walked halfway up the hill to Irun.
Yes, I said, I know the place, cantinas
white, high up, wooded area . . . so
you are returning, extended visit.
Ibañez, John of The Cross, Lorca, yes,
some acquaintance, the last was murdered
one evening at his house, I believe,
beautiful writer, strong in so many ways.
We know nothing of these far-flung places,
Americans; I was required to be
out of uniform, official policy.
Young and dumb—that was me—traveling,

as I see it now, like disembodied
spirit. I was dead—those were my thoughts.
Does an Indian boy cross the border
at Hendaye? I did—into a dreadful
police state, simply to be on my own,
to forget for a while barracks life.
Traveling may shake you from narrow views;
I thought as much, being a reader.
That evening the lady next to me
complained loudly about Americans
and motioned towards where I was sitting.
I picked up a few words, but they seemed
unimportant. "Cervantes cannot be
excluded," I thought. As this fat lady talked,
a Spanish officer across the way
stared at the woman speaking as though
surprised. I had offered American
cigarettes, passed them around—custom—
and that had set her off. Another
miserable blunder. Would this happen
on a spiritual journey, following
the four-day trail? But after a time
the lights on the train were dimmed and we
continued through the night to Madrid.
But, you see, we were also sitting there
on this big hill in eastern Washington
in the lunch room, three of us, laughing.
And I saw that I wasn't getting the job.

Shout Amen!

Shout amen! Christmas in our house and joy
In His birth and truth in His holy name!
Erupting—the holy fire spreading out,
Fervor and strength—while listening round about
The silent, stately trees, the road that came
Our way and turned, the hooting owls, the same
White moon so cold and distant in the sky.

And one step nearer, down the aisle or down
The road, over the years or through the woods,
I was never ever able to go.
Shout amen! I was a traveler within,
Sold on dark storms in pages of all kinds,
Fashioned in the bright world here below.

Christmas Eve!

Upon this Christmas Eve we sing the songs
Of Christmas, gentle words beside a tree
Where ample gifts and childish cares may be,
Where a flourish of lights might well belong.

And what holiday sounds will come as throngs
Of people, at last becoming cheerful, leave
The thoroughfares and freezing cold, all these
Trappings of time while being pushed along.

Moments divided between our idleness
And care, between in-door comfort and large
Blustery days, the fields, the hearth, the circle
Of friends—the season brings it all, the local
Neighborhood, for a while, and lets us charge,
Perhaps, how do you say, our righteousness.

Lamb Without Guile

When this season of merriment and cheer
Becomes last year's occasion, or a smile
That memory awakes but for a while
Before the cold winds of another year,
When the ringing of bells once more is near,
Carols ringing out in a joyful style,
Then blessed Christmas comes—Lamb without guile,
A heavenly light within a childlike tear—
The gift transported in a night of faith,
Recalling omens, travelers above
And the world beneath, but with new found love
Extending, creating, including all
With hope amazingly strong and from a hearth
of light and grace wondrous beyond recall.

Western Gate

Artillery brightens the sky to the north
And on Christmas Eve. We were twenty miles
Or so back of the lines, while to the south
Along the river Han the city of Seoul.

I stood guard as others did while the planes
From a crossroads town lifted into the sky,
Their lights briefly on the fields, on the trains
At the marshaling yard and surrounding cold.

This night at the western gate, meant to be
No more nor less than other nights, was where
The old myths were still a candle flame
Burning at the center of our lives, the name
Holy or Peace writ large—heavy the air
With joy, laughter. There I wanted to be.

Boulevard

The lights of our town were not yet on
But evening and its shadows
And its whispered words were just beyond.
I stood near trees at the center of the boulevard
Letting minutes pass, watching couples turn
And wait, old men going to their places
Down the street, or watching children near the park.

Yesterday these images returned once again
When I saw you crossing the street,
I thought—here is the end of desire,
Autumn breezes scooping up summer's minions,
Summer's leaves, sweeping all into the fields,
Into doorways and walls. The night also
Was bringing its emptiness, its melancholy,
Its unusual price. The film of worlds dissolving
Would be shown once again and again
As the seasons moved and danced and then grew still.
Somehow I, too, was a seed responding
To summer's heat, December's frigid cold.

The Conference

Wisps of fog curling up from Lake Huron
Drifting from the water's edge and causing
Lights to dim or blur along the high
Arc bridge that connects the two parts
Of Sault Ste. Marie

Ojibway Hotel and up on the hill
The university. Yet, timber
And forest and that life
Are only miles out from the thoroughfare.
Many have faced the northern days
And remember harder times.
I give them that. They know the land
And what wind and snow can bring.
They hardly see the ships or hear
The fog horns out on the lakes.
My amazement—why that is just
The stranger in town, and by George,
In a day or two, my kind will retreat
To softer lands.

The conference, though, was a success. They
Usually are. Educators, you might say,
Working in the field, discussing the lay
Of the land, the new crops, the rain
That can be used, simple ways
Of doing things. We also train
Ourselves to respond and also play
The game. But it goes, of course,

With the ways of the world. Yes,
Certainly it was a success.

I can't leave, though, without this,
Pointing out that it was once
Only and Indian town, a stop-over
For the wilder sort paddling up
From Detroit, and a crossroads
Far up north. Schoolcraft was an agent
Here—a writer of books, a man
Who at least tried to understand.
I give him that. He took his swing
And, perhaps, we're better off for it.
Romance, or that attitude that sees gold
Instead of copper, is what I started with
When I arrived at Sault Ste. Marie.
So, I discovered that tourists come
From miles around to buy—can you
Believe it?—fudge. Well, information—
Often, it tells you just where you are
But you still don't know exactly
What it means. The lesson, you see,
Simply comes to an end.

Millennium

Here our millennium is coming to an end.
An appropriate Latin phrase—insert here—
Or something from Carlyle, perhaps *Urn
Burial* with that cold sincerity, or a word
From Alfred Nobel—celebrations all.
The medieval man, callouses and humor,
Gil the Red, his brown-as-a-bun, feudal
Rose, like lentils in a field they grew
And became, unbelievably, what we are:
Merchants, bureaucrats, finely wrapped
Clerics, settlers, students, masked men,
The stuff of chivalry in labs, on playing fields,
Perverts and weaklings, Indian Chiefs, only a few
Compared to the mighty flood, Leviathan.
But *slow*, very likely, became the watch word
In the night of the Black Death, or when flames
Rippled across human dwellings and sent
The people forth into a ravaged countryside.
Who can express a natural upheaval,
Sunrise, a child's hand reaching out
To yours? We "peasants" mark the calendar,
Give new meaning to the word crude,
Pee on monastery walls, and dream
of banquets grandiose and unending.
Let history, weeping tears and groaning,
Lumber on to her quiet outhouse perch.
We will meet the new millennium head on.

Austerlitz Station

Where the trains go south at Austerlitz
Station, Paris, I was saying a last
Farewell to tree-lined streets, life
Caught in stone, outdoor cafes, and
The nave where the great torso of Venus
De Milo stood. Was she not the Trickster
Goddess of this ancient city, guarding
The tower, the artists, the river Seine?
Like a pupil, I remember, I reached out
And touched the marble form, that
Silent breath of an earlier dawn.
No turning back in its constancy or in
Her worldly grace, but yet becoming
In time only a partial thought. But
Enough. Always in the scheme of things
The element of doubt, moments of transition,
Or wonder about what may have been.
Somewhere back in time I was charmed,
Amazed, doubtful about what actually
Occurred when in that early time you
First stood alone before those who placed
You there. Resigned, resolute goddess!
The world has need of your serenity,
Your untroubled depth, your gift
Of patience and calm Mediterranean light

Hermeneutic Circles

This December was another milestone
For me and my son, a faraway son
In Australia, a grandson coming on
Like Gangbusters, even if down under.
The hermeneutic circle never ends,
We add to it somehow with every turn,
Trying to see overall and within,
How each part signifies and how it blends.
Some, I recall, endure the prairie wind,
Or watch in loneliness the silent fields,
Or reflect, as long winter softly comes,
That this might be it, the final run,
simple, strong or valiant— the closing down
Of life, while another circle begins.

The Keys

Walking now forever tired and poor, forever
Being there in the world, forever
Following the thing-in-itself
Forever going through
The raggedy towns
Down the lonely street
Tasting dry and bitter now
The deadening hours turning about
Seeing doors, seeing walls
What can be said to the by-gone years?

Then a merchant of sorts in a book-lined stall
At the end of a crowded, busy day
Smiled and motioned twice to me. "This way,"
He called. "My wares to young and old,
Whoever wants or can partake of these
Our sunny lands"—he gestured in the air—
"And life perhaps more free than what we have,
These shadow towns beside the roads, cities
Sprung from the floor of enterprise, but
For all that, places yet where the heart
And nose are forever clogged. What say you,
Lad, have you found that more is less, that time
Is a stone too difficult to crack?"
My glance was not of confidence and yet
I answered straight, "There is for some
Much wandering, which is what I do,
And who's to say which way I turn,
For I have been about."

His eye caught mine.
"Sir, to say that is to describe us all,
For we invest in the ebb and flow,
In wind and trees, in the future's warmth
As against the cold. Somewhere beyond—
Wandering—it is the dream that spurs us on,
Old horses that we are, but yet I sense,
My boy, that with you there is more
Than the common place." The man spoke soft.
"Aye, there are cages we have seen, you and I,
But let us leave such thoughts deep within."
I recoiled at the words. He caught my arm.
"You are spending now some of what is past,
Some of what clings to you and has always been
Yours to use. I want it now. These keys
Have a price and you have asked for them."

"But, no," I began to protest. "I said
nothing of the sort. I —" But he stopped
my voice, pointing out strange marks, numbers
Engraved, saying that none could be replaced
And each would endure as time went on.
He folded two in my hand as darkness fell
And as though it were a final sale.
What was it that I spent? I never knew,
Though in thought the scene has often reappeared.
So close to nothingness, the words were said
And like pebbles were thrown into a river
Of time. What else? Wandering and my youth
From that street of dreams—were we feathered birds
Discussing flight? Nothing since has been the same.

Early Poems

Navajo Girl of Many Farms

Navajo girl of Many Farms
You ride on blue wings
Why do you fear?
The drop of sun
Is but my hands
Resting at your door
The desert wind
Is but my voice
Saying you are slim
Saying you are strong
The morning light
Is but my song
Singing soft to you
Ride, ride away with me
On your bright, blue wings
We will never return
Navajo girl of Many Farms.

During the Pageant at Medicine Lodge

During the Pageant at Medicine Lodge
One bright line this—recollected but passing away,
like a leaf that escaped the fire; it
appears still golden, life-inhabited,
imbued with light, with the filtered hush
of deep forests.

During the Pageant at Medicine Lodge
Later it seemed that the redman had been only a dream
on paper, an elegant falsehood strutting
before pioneers, a dancing image fading
deeper into the forests, into the wild streams,
into earth itself. They were never real!
They sang—bird-like, bear-like, like wind,
rustle of trees, crickets—and were no more.

During the Pageant at Medicine Lodge
Conversational scraps and ideas. "A few might have
survived," I said. I wanted to say,
"You and I." But why stab at thin air.
The past survives in the mind. On that
particular day in southern Kansas *no Indians
were there*. It was a jolly ride, it was dusty
and hot, it was fun, but the Indians,
whoever they were, did not arrive.

Now the People Have the Light

Now the people have the light
But time must pass, days of autumn
While the deer drink at the pool

Visions gathered by proud men
Will not affect the light, the summer rains
Must fall on a world of leaves

The swarms of small life on wings
Must find the lake, the evening birds
Bring back the songs of youth

Steaming riverbeds on the Great Plains
Must sigh for the lizard and receive
In dark sand the wayward stars

Mountain peaks high over the land
Must keep the watch through all the years
For now the people have the light

Changing of the Guard

Why do you hold the flag so high
Old fellow of the Sac and Fox?
Those stars were never in your sky

From times past we have gone to war
Now the young are speaking new words
So be it. They have done so before

And it must come to them, the flag
If they take it from these useless hands
It must still be there, high up and strong

Grandfather, or whatever you are
You have spoken your sold-out words
To your strength I cannot reply

I know only that the time has come
When gratitude for treachery is gone
When kisses for the greedy are unclean

When I take the flag, old man
It will be but to honor the forgotten dead
Those who died for the Indian dream

Let no more be said, my son
On this matter we are of one mind
In my old time way I pass it on to you

Grandma Fire

Grandma Fire
Old and naked in the dawn
No answer sings out from your lips
Only the kettle deep
Ferment of tribes—fires that keep
To the edge of night
Old hands like roots
But seedlings to life—birds to wing!

Grandma Fire
Every way on that time
Eyes appeared from every stream
People seemed to flee
Headstrong the wind—strong the fire
From every hand it was
Crisscrossing the land
And gone it was—birds to wing!

Grandma Fire
Always ours for the good
The songs were ours to sing
Twisting, barking in the flood
From every forest—from deeper spring
Where rooted everlasting
The Indian heart
And ever uplifting—birds to wing!

The Spirit Craft

How beautiful and calm how crimson pale
And sweet the dawn upon God's mountainside
Tomorrow is here if we but decide
To see it through step lightly through the veil
From darkness to the day let spirit sail
Across the night and feel the sway and glide
Of spirit craft when word and deed provide
The passage sure upward into the light

Today is now a yesterday a line
Unbroken from joyous youth through a dream
Of enfeebled age a spring and waterfall
A river winding broad and deep across the plain
A memory of mountains and a stream
That always was from out of heaven's wall

Their Cone-Like Cabins

"Their-cone-like cabins," she said
That poetess of Hartford
Who gently took her stick
Sweetly stirred the ashes
Of Hiawatha's book

"Ye say they went away," she sang
The Winnebago certainly did
About seven times
And at every stopping place
The same old words

As long as rivers flow
And grass shall grow
The strong will stuff their pockets
Usually break wind
As they calmly watch you go

Memo

It would be painful to interfere
To set the locust among the corn
To set the tiger upon the lamb
To set man against fellow man
To adjust the conquest, oversee the plan
To let a nation fall and proclaim
White death and cold and bitterness
While leaders like dry twigs are cast
Into the fire by those who rub
Their hands and smile . . .
It would be painful to interfere

Time was the Trail Went Deep

Time was the trail went deep
From the granite ledge of the Verdigris
On west to rivers flat
And a rolling sea of grass

We followed the Arkansas to New Town
Of the Creeks and veered off
To low hills in the north
Where we camped in those final days

Having walked to never look back
Having talked to carry through
We disbanded and were no more
To choose finally is the Indian way

But time was the trail went deep
Into a green and vibrant land

First Book Awards For Poetry

Established in 1992 in conjunction with the Returning The Gift Festival, The North American Native Authors Poetry Award is given for a first book by a Native writer. Named the Diane Decorah Award in memory of a Native writer and supporter of other Native authors, its winners published by The Greenview Review Press are:

1992   Gloria Bird *Full Moon On The Reservation*

1993   Kimberly Blaeser *Trailing You*

1994   Tiffany Midge *Outlaws, Renegades and Saints*

1995   Denise Sweet *Songs For Discharming*

1996   Charles G. Ballard *Winter Count Poems*

1997   Deborah A. Miranda *Indian Cartography*